California Notary Public Exam

"You never fail until you stop trying" - Albert Einstein

For inquiries;
info@xmprep.com

California Notary Public Exam #1

Test Taking Tips

- ☐ Take a deep breath and relax
- ☐ Read directions carefully
- ☐ Read the questions thoroughly
- ☐ Make sure you understand what is being asked
- ☐ Go over all of the choices before you answer
- ☐ Paraphrase the question
- ☐ Eliminate the options you know are wrong
- ☐ Check your work
- ☐ Think positively and do your best

Table of Contents

TEST DIRECTION

DIRECTIONS

Read the questions carefully and then choose the ONE best answer to each question.

Be sure to allocate your time carefully so you are able to complete the entire test within the testing session. You may go back and review your answers at any time.

You may use any available space in your test booklet for scratch work.

Questions in this booklet are not actual test questions but they are the samples for commonly asked questions.

This test aims to cover all topics which may appear on the actual test. However some topics may not be covered.

Studying this booklet will be preparing you for the actual test. It will not guarantee improving your test score but it will help you pass your exam on the first attempt.

Some useful tips for answering multiple choice questions;

- Start with the questions that you can easily answer.

- Underline the keywords in the question.

- Be sure to read all the choices given.

- Watch for keywords such as NOT, always, only, all, never, completely.

- Do not forget to answer every question.

1

According to the California laws, what is the fee for verifying any nomination document or circulator's affidavit?

A) $3

B) $7

C) $15

D) No fee is required

2

Which of the following is the requirement to be a Notary Public in California?

A) Passing a background check

B) Passing a written examination prescribed by the Secretary of State

C) Satisfactorily completing a course of study approved by the Secretary of State

D) All of the above

3

An **eNotary** is a Notary Public who notarizes documents electronically by using a digital signature and digital notary seal to notarize digital documents and validate with a digital certificate.

Which of the following about eNotary is/are correct?

A) An eNotary Public must not engage in the unauthorized practice of law.

B) An eNotary Public must use the same certificates as used in paper-based notarizations.

C) An eNotary Public must not choose the notarial certificates to be completed in a transaction.

D) All of the above

4

A notary who is appointed under the name of Mary K. Jones may sign as which of the following?

A) M.K. Jones

B) M. Jones

C) Mary K. Jones

D) All of the above

CONTINUE ▶

5

Affiant is a person who swears to an affidavit, which is a written statement used as evidence in court.

If an affiant swears falsely, which of the following can he/she be prosecuted for?

A) Fraud

B) Forgery

C) Perjury

D) Misrepresentation

6

Which of the following appoints and commissions a notary public?

A) Attorney General

B) Governor Authority

C) Secretary of State

D) Office of General Services

7

Which of the following refers the person who is a signer of and party to a document?

A) Surety

B) Principal

C) Witness

D) Signing Agent

8

Certificates of acknowledgment or proof are not entitled to be read in evidence or recorded in this state if they are made in a foreign country other than which of the following?

A) United Kingdom

B) Canada

C) Guam

D) Mexico

CONTINUE ▶

9

A **mobile notary** is a notary public who is mobile and travels to clients.

Which of the following about mobile notaries are correct?

A) No special training is required to become a mobile notary.

B) Most of the jobs available to mobile notaries are loan signings

C) To become a mobile notary, you must first become a commissioned notary public in your state.

D) All of the above

10

Which of the following can prevent an individual from becoming a notary public?

A) Holding another public office

B) Being a commissioned military officer

C) Being a retired public employee

D) Being a minor

11

A JURAT is added to which of the following?

A) Certificate

B) Affidavit

C) Affirmation

D) Attestation

12

A **legislature** is a deliberative assembly with authority to make laws for a political entity such as a country or city.

Which of the following is the name given to the laws which are passed by legislatures?

A) Bill

B) Statute

C) Contract

D) Code

13

A notary public is NOT allowed to administer an oath to which of the following?

A) Himself

B) Public officials

C) Family members

D) Military officers

An **electronic document** refers to any information in digital form.

Which of the following about the electronic documents of eNotary is not true?

A) Electronic Documets are system generated documents created by filling in form fields.

B) Adobe Acrobat and Microsoft Word are the most common electronic documets of eNotary

C) The Electronic Notary may not keep an electronic register of electronic documents of each act performed.

D) Electronic Documet refers to any information that is created, generated, sent, communicated, received, or stored by electronic means.

If a California notary willfully fails to provide access to the sequential journal of notarial acts when requested by a peace officer, he or she will be subject to a civil penalty of which of the following?

A) No more than $500

B) No more than $750

C) No more than $1,000

D) No more than $2,500

Which of the following is a crime, typically one involving violence, punishable by imprisonment in a state prison?

A) Felony

B) Perjury Crime

C) Misdemeanor

D) Criminal Offense

A person who communicates by telephone or mail in a manner to cause annoyance or alarm is guilty of which of the following?

A) Felony

B) Assault

C) Battery

D) Harassment

18

If a person has been convicted of a felony, he may not be appointed as a notary public in which of the following?

A) Any state of the United States

B) The county of jurisdiction

C) Any place in the world

D) Some states of the United States

19

"**Crime**" means which of the following?

A) Attempt to commit a crime

B) Aiding and abetting of a crime

C) Solicitation to commit a crime

D) All of the above

20

Which of the following is/are the reasons to deny a Notary Public applicant in California?

A) Conviction of a felony

B) Failure to disclose any conviction

C) Conviction of a disqualifying lesser offense

D) All of the above

21

Which of the following documents does not require a seal?

A) The subdivision map

B) The certificate of veterans

C) The circulator's affidavit

D) The change of venue

22

When taking an oath what should the signer do?

A) Must raise right hand

B) Must pay an extra fee

C) Must repeat oath

D) It is not required to raise the right hand.

23

In California, each notary public is required to have and to use a seal.

Which of the following is/are correct about notary seal requirements in California?

A) It can be circular not over two inches in diameter.
B) It contains the expiration date of the notary public's commission.
C) It can be a rectangular form of no more than one inch in width by two and one-half inches in length.
D) All of the above.

24

Which of the following term is not defined correctly?

A) Affirmation is a notarial act which is legally equivalent to an oath.
B) Appointment is a notarial act which doesn't necessarily require principal to sign in front of notary.
C) Attestation is the completion of a certificate by a notary who has performed a notarial act.
D) Applicant is an individual who seeks appointment for the first time or reappointment to the office of notary public.

25

Notary Bond is a financial guarantee Notaries purchase from a surety company to protect the public from mistakes that notaries make while performing notarial act.

California law requires every notary public to file an official bond in the amount of $15,000.

Which of the following is/are correct about Notary Public Bond in California?

A) It is not an insurance policy for the notary public.

B) It is designed only to provide a limited source of funds for paying claims against the notary public.

C) The notary public may be required to reimburse the bonding company for sums paid by the company because of misconduct or negligence of the notary public.

D) All of the above

26

Which of the following is the process of taking an argument between people or groups to a court of law?

A) Compromise

B) Litigation

C) Protestation

D) Perjury

27

Ryan is a notary and he was called to notarize several documents for his cousin Brian. When he arrived, Ryan learned that Brian's license had expired.

Which of the following method of identification can not be used by Ryan?

A) Ryan's personal knowledge of Brian

B) Brian's United States passport

C) Two credible witnesses whom Ryan does not know

D) Single credible witness whom Ryan knows

28

Which of the following is the prime duty of a Notary Public?

A) To serve the public as an impartial witness when relevant documents are signed; administer oaths, and take proof and acknowledgment of written instruments.

B) To attest to the genuineness of any deeds or writings to render them available as evidence of the facts therein contained.

C) To take acknowledge of or proof of the execution of an instrument by the client.

D) To attest to the genuineness of notice, in that one who is entitled to notice of a fact, will thus be bound by acquiring knowledge of it.

29

Within how many days a notary public is required to notify California Secretary of State of any change of business or residence address in writing, by certifed mail or any other means of physical delivery that provides a receipt?

A) 7 days

B) 10 days

C) 15 days

D) 30 days

30

Which of the following happens if an appointee does not file his oath of office within the specified period?

A) The fee is refunded.

B) The appointment is revoked.

C) The appointee is guilty of a misdemeanor.

D) The appointee can not apply for a new appointment for at least one month.

31

Which of the following is a crime punishable with death in California?

A) Perjury

B) Felony

C) Misdemeanor

D) Official misconduct

32

The origination of a useless certificate and the collection of a fee therefore after receipt of notice that such practices must be discontinued justifies which of the following finding?

A) Misfeasance

B) Malpractice

C) Insubordination

D) Misconduct

33

Which of the following must a Notary do?

A) Keep a copy of every document notarized.

B) Keep the stamp and journal under his direct control

C) Send the copy of the notarized document to the State

D) All of the above

34

Which of the following refers to the person who has authority to sign for another?

A) Principal

B) Surety

C) Witness

D) Attorney in Fact

35

The **oath** is a solemn promise, often invoking a divine witness, regarding one's future action or behavior.

For an oath to be effective, in which form must it be?

A) Oral

B) Written

C) Witnessed

D) All of the above

10

CONTINUE ▶

36

State of _____

County of _____

The location where the notarial act takes place is usually stated in the format given above at the beginning of the notarial certificate.

Which of the following terms is used to refer to the state and county where a notarization takes place?

A) Location
B) Place
C) Site
D) Venue

37

Which of the following powers can a notary public possess?

A) Taking acknowledgments
B) Taking verifications and proofs
C) Administering oaths and affirmations
D) All of the above

38

Which one below is applicable for taking an acknowledgment and swearing two witnesses?

A) The notary can not charge for it.
B) The notary can charge if he travels to the client.
C) The notary can charge for it.
D) The notary should not charge to elderly.

39

If an affiant swears falsely, for which of the following he may be prosecuted?

A) Fraud against law
B) Forgery of the official document
C) Committing perjury
D) Counterfeiting

40

It is a certificate issued by the Secretary of State that proves the authenticity of a notary's signature and seal. It is proof of authentication for notarized documents in countries that abide by the 1961 Hague Convention Abolishing the Requirement of Legalization for Foreign Public Documents.

Which of the following is explained above?

A) Apostille
B) Notarial Certificate
C) Certification Authority (CA)
D) Acknowledgment Certificate

41

Each state sets the fees for notaries public. Under which of the following circumstances is a notary public permitted to receive a higher payment for a service than generally allowed by law?

A) Under no circumstance
B) When the workload is too much
C) When extra expenses are incurred
D) When extraordinary circumstances demand it

42

It is a formal written enactment of a legislative authority that governs a state, city or country.

Which of the following is defined above?

A) The Secretary of State
B) Courts of record
C) Statute
D) Tradition

43

Which of the following does a notary public have the authority to lawfully do?

A) Execute a will and trust
B) Take the acknowledgment to a legal instrument in which he has a financial report
C) Take the acknowledgment of his constituent
D) Take the acknowledgment of a third party

44

To demonstrate genuineness by signing as a witness, which of the following must the notary public do?

A) Authenticate the instrument.

B) Endorse the instrument.

C) Attest the instrument.

D) Certify the instrument.

45

CLASS OF FELONIES

K : Life imprisonment or death

L : 25 years or more

M : Less than 25 years but 10 or more years

N : Less than 10 years but 5 or more years

O : Less than 5 years but more than 1 year

A notary who executes a false certificate with the intention to defraud or deceive with the knowledge that it contains a false statement is guilty of which class of felonies given above?

A) L

B) M

C) O

D) N

46

Which of the following can a notary public do?

A) Ensure that the certificate is appropriate and complete.

B) Ensure that his printed or typed name appears in the certificate.

C) Ensure that the information in his certificate matches the facts of the notarial act.

D) All of the above

47

An attorney will be prohibited from the office of the notary public in which of the following cases?

A) If he is a resident but not a member of the bar

B) If he is a non-resident and not admitted to practice in the courts of record of this state

C) If he is admitted to practice in the courts of record of this state and moves out of state

D) If he is a non-resident only maintaining an office within this state

48

Which of the following determines the number of notary public in an area?

A) County clerk
B) The legislature
C) The Secretary of State
D) The city civil service commission (CSC)

49

A **false certificate** is when a person is guilty of issuing official certificates or other official written instruments, and with intent to defraud, deceive or injure another person.

A notary public who knowingly makes a false certificate may be prosecuted for which of the following?

A) Malfeasance
B) Forgery of the official document
C) Misconduct
D) A misdemeanor

50

CLASS OF FELONIES

A : Life imprisonment or death

B : 25 years or more

C : Less than 25 years but 10 or more years

D : Less than 10 years but 5 or more years

E : Less than 5 years but more than 1 year

Forgery is the process of making, adapting, or imitating objects, statistics, or documents with the intent to deceive for the sake of altering the public perception.

A person guilty of forgery in the second degree is guilty of which class of a felony?

A) B
B) C
C) D
D) E

51

Which of the below is a debt instrument, secured by the collateral of specified real estate property, that the borrower is obliged to pay back with a predetermined set of payments?

A) Conveyance
B) Mortgage
C) Escrow
D) Lease

52

A notary public can not do which of the following?

A) He can not place his seal on a different page than his signature.

B) He can not loan or give his seal to anyone else.

C) He can not perform a notary act after his commission expires.

D) All of the above

53

Signature

The most critical of the five notary-specific elements on a notarized document is the notary signature. By signing the notary certificate, a notary is verifying that the venue, notary commission expiration date, and the notary certificate are true and correct.

In which color must the signature of the notary public be?

A) Blue

B) Black

C) Blue or black

D) Any color

54

Felony is a crime, typically one involving violence regarded as more severe than a misdemeanor, and usually punishable by imprisonment for more than one year or by death.

A felony in another jurisdiction, for the purpose of disqualification from the office of notary public, depends on all of the following except which one?

A) Whether the executive pardon was received

B) The exact nature of the crime

C) The statute upon which the conviction is based

D) If reciprocity exists

55

A **will** is an official document that says what a person wants to be done with his assets after his death.

Which of the following is the person named in a will to carry out a particular act on the estates?

A) Executor

B) Intestate

C) Administrator

D) Surrogate

56

It is taken orally, with an attorney asking questions and the deponent (the individual being questioned) answering while a court reporter or tape recorder (or sometimes both) records the testimony.

Which of the following is explained above?

A) Testament

B) Deposition

C) Subpoena

D) Deposition testimony

57

Which of the following is the act of recognizing the existence of a signed agreement as evidence of one's intention that the agreement is binding and in full force?

A) Acceptance

B) Acknowledgment

C) Notarial act

D) Transaction

58

Notaries must complete journal entries at the time of notarization. Which items must always be in the journal?

A) Date, fees, time, type of document

B) Date, type of document, fees

C) Fees, document date, the name of the signer

D) Date, time, fees, thumbprint, the address of the signer

59

Credible witness is an individual who is personally known to the notary.

Which of the following applies to credible witness?

A) The notary believes the individual is not a beneficiary of the transaction.

B) The notary believes the individual is honest and reliable for confirming to the notary the identity of another individual.

C) Both A and B

D) Neither A nor B

A Notary Public is an official of integrity appointed by state government to serve the public as an impartial witness in performing a variety of official fraud-deterrent acts related to the signing of relevant documents.

Which of the following terms defines a notary public BEST?

A) Amicus curiae
B) Ministerial official
C) Legal counselor
D) Judicial official

Section 1

#	Answer	Topic	Subtopic	#	Answer	Topic	Subtopic	#	Answer	Topic	Subtopic	#	Answer	Topic	Subtopic
1	D	TFA	SFA2	16	D	TFA	SFA2	31	B	TFA	SFA2	46	D	TAB	SAB1
2	D	TFA	SFA2	17	D	TAA	SAA1	32	B	TAA	SAA1	47	B	TAA	SAA1
3	D	TAB	SAB3	18	A	TAA	SAA2	33	B	TAB	SAB1	48	C	TAA	SAA2
4	C	TAB	SAB2	19	D	TAA	SAA2	34	D	TAA	SAA1	49	B	TAA	SAA1
5	C	TAB	SAB1	20	D	TFA	SFA2	35	A	TAB	SAB1	50	C	TAA	SAA1
6	C	TAA	SAA1	21	A	TAA	SAA1	36	D	TAA	SAA1	51	B	TAA	SAA1
7	B	TAA	SAA1	22	D	TAB	SAB1	37	D	TAB	SAB1	52	D	TAA	SAA2
8	B	TAA	SAA2	23	D	TFA	SFA2	38	C	TAB	SAB1	53	B	TAB	SAB1
9	D	TAB	SAB1	24	B	TAA	SAA1	39	C	TAB	SAB1	54	D	TAA	SAA1
10	D	TAB	SAB1	25	D	TFA	SFA2	40	A	TAA	SAA1	55	A	TAA	SAA1
11	A	TAB	SAB2	26	B	TAA	SAA1	41	A	TAB	SAB2	56	D	TAA	SAA1
12	B	TAA	SAA1	27	A	TAB	SAB1	42	C	TAA	SAA2	57	B	TAB	SAB1
13	A	TAB	SAB2	28	A	TAB	SAB2	43	C	TAB	SAB1	58	A	TAA	SAA1
14	C	TAB	SAB3	29	D	TFA	SFA2	44	C	TAB	SAB1	59	C	TAB	SAB1
15	A	TAB	SAB1	30	B	TAA	SAA1	45	C	TAB	SAB1	60	B	TAB	SAB1

Topics & Subtopics

Code	Description	Code	Description
SAA	General Knowledge	SAB2	Duties
SAA1	Basic Concepts	SAB3	eNotary
SAA2	Local Issues	SFA	Legal
SAB	Legal	SFA2	Rules
SAB1	Rules		

CONTINUE ▶

TEST DIRECTION

DIRECTIONS

Read the questions carefully and then choose the ONE best answer to each question.

Be sure to allocate your time carefully so you are able to complete the entire test within the testing session. You may go back and review your answers at any time.

You may use any available space in your test booklet for scratch work.

Questions in this booklet are not actual test questions but they are the samples for commonly asked questions.

This test aims to cover all topics which may appear on the actual test. However some topics may not be covered.

Studying this booklet will be preparing you for the actual test. It will not guarantee improving your test score but it will help you pass your exam on the first attempt.

Some useful tips for answering multiple choice questions;

- Start with the questions that you can easily answer.

- Underline the keywords in the question.

- Be sure to read all the choices given.

- Watch for keywords such as NOT, always, only, all, never, completely.

- Do not forget to answer every question.

CONTINUE ▶

1

Sovereign citizens are "anti-government extremists who believe that even though they physically reside in this country, they are separate or 'sovereign' from the United States."

Sovereigns believe they don't need driver's licenses, license plates, vehicle registrations, or insurance to traverse the country's highways.

Which of the following about Sovereign citizens is/are true?

A) They do not recognize U.S. currency and maintain that they are "free of any legal constraints"

B) Sovereign citizens believe that natural citizens are not subject to any United States federal law, including being subject to the jurisdiction of federal courts

C) Many sovereign citizens believe that only white men have rights because only the Constitution and the Bill of Rights apply, not any subsequent amendments

D) All of the above

2

If a California notary willfully states as true any material fact that she knows to be false, then she will be subject to a civil penalty of which of the following?

A) No more than $500

B) No more than $2,500

C) No more than $7,500

D) No more than $10,000

3

Who does the court administer to the estate of a person that has passed away without leaving a will?

A) Executor

B) Intestate

C) Administrator

D) Surrogate

4

An **oath** is a solemn declaration made according to law, to tell the truth, or to take a specific action.

Which of the following is the equivalent of an oath?

A) Attestation

B) Affirmation

C) Testimony

D) Personal Chattel   CONTINUE ▶

5

Any person not appointed and who conveys that he is a notary public may be prosecuted for which of the following?

A) Misconduct

B) A misdemeanor

C) Perjury

D) A felony

6

Which of the following is the fee to certify a copy of a power of attorney under Section 4307 of the Probate Code?

A) $5

B) $7

C) $15

D) $20

7

Which of the following term is not defined correctly?

A) Revocation means the termination of a notary's commission for a period of time.

B) "Notarial certificate" and "certificate" mean the portion of a notarized record that is completed by the notary.

C) Credible witness is an individual that the notary believes the individual to be honest and reliable.

D) Commission is the empowerment to perform notarial acts and the written evidence of authority to perform those acts.

8

Notaries are required to administer oaths in the manner and form prescribed by which of the following?

A) Real Property Law

B) Judiciary Law

C) Public Officers Law

D) Civil Practice Law and Rules

9

By making or giving a notarial certificate, which of the following can the notary certify?

A) The signer was personally known.
B) The signer produced satisfactory evidence of identity.
C) The signer or subscribing witness personally appeared before the Notary Public.
D) All of the above

10

A California Notary Public is required to keep one active sequential journal at a time of all acts performed as a notary public.

Which of the following is included in California notary journal?

A) Date, time and type of each offcial act
B) The signature of each person whose signature is being notarized.
C) A statement that the identity of a person making an acknowledgment or taking an oath or affirmation was based on "satisfactory evidence"
D) All of the above

11

Which of the below is not the duty of the notary public?

A) Swearing to an affirmation
B) Signing off on an acknowledgment
C) Signing off on a deposition
D) Formation of a will

12

What should a California Notary Public do if he is in doubt as to whether or not to notarize a document?

A) Notarize the document
B) Seek the advice of an attorney
C) Seek the advice of county clerk
D) Refuse notarizing the document

13

If a notary willfully fails to notify the California Secretary of State of a name change, she will be punishable as an infraction by a fine of which of the following?

A) No more than $50
B) No more than $500
C) No more than $1,000
D) No more than $2,500

14

A notary public is considered a public officer appointed by a state government. The primary job duty of a notary is to help prevent fraud by witnessing the signing of documents and verifying their authenticity.

Which of the following can a notary not do?

A) Administer Oaths
B) Perform Marriages
C) Charge for his services
D) Take an acknowledgment on a conveyance

15

When a notary makes or gives a notarial certificate, which of the following can he certify?

A) The signer was not under the influence.
B) The signer voluntarily signed the document.
C) The signer understood the nature and consequence of the transaction.
D) All of the above

16

An **ex parte decision** is one decided by a judge without requiring all of the parties to the controversy to be present.

Which of the following is an ex parte statement?

A) Deposition
B) Acknowledgment
C) Affidavit
D) Conveyance

17

If a notary is unable to communicate with a client, then which of the following should the notary do?

A) Refuse the notarization
B) Report the issue to the Secretay of State
C) Report the client to Immigration authorities
D) Notarize the documents

18

When a regulation states 30 days, what does it mean?

A) Calendar days
B) Business days
C) Both A and B
D) Neither A nor B

19

The purpose of an **acknowledgment** is for a signer, whose identity has been verified, to declare to a Notary or notarial officer that he or she has willingly signed a document.

Which of the following is the thing to be known by the notary in taking an acknowledgment?

A) The facts

B) The reason

C) The truth of the acknowledgment

D) The identity of the maker is the same as the executor

20

The primary job duty of a notary is to help prevent fraud by witnessing the signing of documents and verifying their authenticity.

Which of the following is a notary public allowed to do?

A) Making advertisement

B) Drawing up a deed

C) Giving legal advice

D) Executing an acknowledgment of a will

21

It is the person who signs a record for the purpose of being a witness to the principal's execution of record.

Which of the following is explained above?

A) Credible witness

B) Subscribing witness

C) Witness to a Will

D) None of the above

22

It is a notary's certificate evidencing the administration of an oath or affirmation.

Which of the following is defined above?

A) Jurat

B) Principal

C) Record

D) Director

23

Every person appointed to be a notary public in California must execute an official bond in the sum of how many dollars?

A) $5,000

B) $10,000

C) $15,000

D) $50,000

24

In notarial practice, which of the following conditions for a deponent is the most significant?

A) The deponent is who he says he is

B) The deponent is competent

C) The deponent can pay the fee

D) The deponent understands the ramifications of all he is swearing to

25

There are many requirements to be a notary public. Because of which of the following a candidate for the office of notary public cannot be appointed?

A) Drunk driving

B) Misdemeanor

C) Possessing burglar's instruments

D) Traffic Offenses

26

Sometimes notaries elect to file their signatures so that it makes verification easier.

A certificate of an official character is issued when a notary wants to practice in which of the following?

A) County

B) City

C) States

D) Country

27

If a California Notary Public willfully surrenders the notary public's seal to any person not authorized to possess it, he or she will be guilty of which of the following?

A) Perjury

B) Misdemeanor

C) Official misconduct

D) None of the above

28

If it is expected for a notary to sign documents outside her county of residence, she may elect to file her oath of office and signature with which of the following?

A) Other county clerks

B) The Secretary of State

C) The State Supreme Court

D) No one needs to know

CONTINUE ▶

29

If a notary public fails to administer an oath, he will be found guilty of which of the following?

A) Felony

B) Misdemeanor

C) Remove from office

D) None of the above

30

The Office of notary public is one of great antiquity and historical significance. It is unclear, however, when or where the first public notary was formally appointed. One of the earliest references to a notary dates back to the time of Cicero.

According to the passage given above, when and where was the office of notary public established?

A) Ancient Greece

B) Medieval England

C) The Roman Empire

D) Colonial America

31

Notary seal must be kept in a locked and secured area, under the direct and exclusive control of the notary public.

Which of the following is/are correct about notary seal requirements in California?

A) It should contain the State Seal and the words "Notary Public".

B) It should contain the name of the notary public as shown on the commission.

C) It should contain the name of the county where the oath of office and notary public bond are on file.

D) All of the above.

32

Which of the following is a requirement to be appointed as a notary public?

A) United States citizenship

B) Residence of the state

C) Having a place of business in the state

D) Registering as a voter

CONTINUE ▶

33

Which of the following defines the agreements made between two parties to do or not to do certain things for legal consideration, whereby each acquires a right to what the other owns?

A) Lien
B) Contract
C) Bill of sale
D) Consideration

34

If an individual wishes to sue a non-resident notary public, the summons may be served upon which of the following?

A) County clerk
B) Attorney general
C) Secretary of State
D) Notary only

35

When is a county clerk's authentication of notary's authority obtained?

A) When the document specifies a land conveyance
B) When the document is to be used in the County
C) When the document requires such authentication
D) When the document is used outside the State

36

An **indictment** is a formal accusation that a person has committed a crime.

If a notary charges for services more than the law allows him, he is subject to indictment. Which of the following would he not be indicted with?

A) Criminal contempt
B) Treble damages
C) Criminal prosecution
D) Felony

37

If the lessee of a safe deposit box doesn't pay the rental fee or doesn't empty the box after the prescribed period by the law, the box may be opened by a notary accompanied by which of the following?

A) Locksmith
B) County clerk
C) Bank guard
D) Bank officer

38

A **duly qualified** notary public is considered capable of performing notarial duties by which of the following?

A) Rules of the Secretary of State
B) Rules of the Governor
C) Dictates of his conscience
D) The law

39

It is a "lesser" criminal act in some common law legal systems. It is considered a crime of low seriousness. Mostly it is punished with monetary fines.

A person who depicts himself as a notary will be guilty of the crime described above.

Which of the following is the name given to this crime?

A) Misdemeanor

B) Felony

C) Harassment

D) Perjury

40

Which of the following terms is not defined correctly?

A) Affiant is the person who is a signer of and party to a document.

B) Statutory Fee is the charge prescribed by law for services.

C) Signature by Proxy is the signature made on behalf of a principal by a Notary.

D) Protest is the act in which a Notary certifies that a signer did not receive payment for a negotiable instrument.

41

It is an act or behavior that gravely violates the sentiment or accepted standard of the community. It is an act contrary to expected standards of honesty, morality, or integrity.

Which of the following is defined above?

A) Crime

B) Moral turpitude

C) Attestation

D) Official misconduct

42

If the notary is notarizing a document for a personal friend, which of the following may be included in the journal?

A) Fee for the notary

B) Right thumbprint of signer

C) Date, time and type of the document notarized.

D) All of the above

43

Which of the following is the name given to the section of the state law which requires certain contracts MUST be in writing or partially complied with to be enforceable at law?

A) Proof clause
B) Contract law
C) Common law
D) Statute of frauds

44

Which of the following is not correct?

A) The deed is a document by which a person conveys (transfers) real property.
B) Affiant is the person making an affidavit.
C) A felony is a lesser crime than a misdemeanor.
D) The transfer, surrender, or assignment of any interest in real property is called a conveyance.

45

Notary public fees are determined by which of the following?

A) The law
B) Each notary sets his fee
C) The fee is determined by agreement
D) States set maximum allowable charges for standard notary costs, and notaries can charge any amount up to that maximum.

46

It is an act where a Principal signer signs a document in the presence of a Subscribing Witness. Then subscribing witness swears under Oath before a Notary Public that the principal signer signed the document in their presence.

Which of the following is defined above?

A) Attestation
B) Affirmation
C) A Proof of Execution
D) Verification or proof

47

Which of the following performs an attestation?

A) Attorney
B) Notary
C) Deponent
D) Witness

48

Which of the following is the process of giving sworn evidence and document used as testimony in court proceedings?

A) Write
B) Instrument
C) Deposition
D) Subpoena

49

An individual might become a notary public if his appointment was revoked by failure to file within the specified period by which of the following?

A) Reapplying

B) Paying a fee

C) Reapplying and paying a fee

D) Reapplying and passing the qualifying exam

50

A **county clerk** is an elected county official who is responsible for local elections and maintaining public records.

The signature and seal of a county clerk upon a certificate of the official character of a notary public may be in which of the following format?

A) Printed

B) Photographed

C) Engraved

D) All of the above

51

If a notary public practices any fraudulent activity or deceitful act in his performance duties he can be convicted of which of the following?

A) Misconduct

B) A misdemeanor

C) Malpractice

D) A felony

52

A **subscribing witness** is one who sees writing executed or hears it acknowledged, and at the request of the party thereupon signs his name as a witness.

Who is the subscribing witness to any instrument verified or acknowledged before a notary public?

A) Notary public

B) Constituent

C) Affiant

D) Maker

CONTINUE ▶

53

In the law of the United States, a **deposition** is the (out-of-court) oral testimony of a witness. Which of the following is a name given to a deposition?

A) Affair
B) Attestator
C) Deponent
D) Depositor

54

The jurisdiction of a notary public broadens throughout which of the following?

A) United States
B) State only
C) County of residence
D) City of residence

55

When a Notary changes a business address to a new county within the state, which of the following must the notary do?

A) Inform the Secretary of State of the address change
B) File a new oath of office and amendment to the Notary's bond.
C) Change the name of the county in the Notary's seal.
D) All of the above

56

Attestation is the act of showing or evidence showing that something is accurate and factual. It refers to a third party recognition of a documented agreement's validity.

Which of the following performs the attestation?

A) Attorney
B) Witness
C) Deponent
D) Litigant

CONTINUE ▶

57

A **stockholder** is an individual, group, or organization that holds one or more shares in a company, and in whose name the share certificate is issued. It's also known as the shareholder.

Which of the following may a notary who is a stockholder of a corporation do?

A) Not protesting for the non-acceptance of negotiable instruments owned by the corporation

B) Not protesting for the non-payment of negotiable instruments owned by the corporation

C) Protesting for the non-acceptance and non-payment of negotiable instruments owned or held for collection by that corporation

D) Protesting for the non-acceptance and non-payment of negotiable instruments held for collection by the corporation

58

If a person does not file his oath of office within the prescribed time, his appointment is revoked.

Which of the following given below does he have to do if his appointment is revoked?

A) Paying the fee

B) Reapplying and paying the fee

C) Reapplying only

D) Passing the examination

59

The **impediment** is a hindrance or obstruction in doing something.

Which of the following is a legal impediment to a person being appointed to the office of a notary public?

A) Illegally using or carrying a pistol

B) Receiving or having criminal possession of stolen property

C) Unlawful possession of a habit-forming narcotic drug

D) All of the above

60

Making an oath, stating under oath or making a solemn promise to a Supreme Being.

Which of the following is defined above?

A) Will

B) Swear

C) Affirmation

D) Attestation

Section 2

#	Answer	Topic	Subtopic	#	Answer	Topic	Subtopic	#	Answer	Topic	Subtopic	#	Answer	Topic	Subtopic
1	D	TAA	SAA1	16	C	TAA	SAA1	31	D	TFA	SFA2	46	C	TAB	SAB1
2	D	TFA	SFA2	17	A	TAA	SAA1	32	A	TAB	SAB1	47	D	TAA	SAA1
3	C	TAA	SAA1	18	A	TAB	SAB1	33	B	TAA	SAA1	48	C	TAB	SAB1
4	B	TAB	SAB1	19	B	TAA	SAA1	34	C	TAA	SAA2	49	C	TAB	SAB1
5	B	TAA	SAA1	20	A	TAB	SAB1	35	D	TAB	SAB1	50	D	TAB	SAB2
6	C	TFA	SFA2	21	B	TAB	SAB1	36	A	TAB	SAB1	51	B	TAB	SAB1
7	A	TAA	SAA1	22	A	TCB	SCB2	37	D	TAB	SAB2	52	A	TAA	SAA1
8	D	TAB	SAB1	23	C	TFA	SFA2	38	D	TAB	SAB1	53	C	TAB	SAB1
9	D	TAA	SAA1	24	A	TAB	SAB1	39	A	TAA	SAA1	54	B	TAA	SAA2
10	D	TFA	SFA2	25	C	TAA	SAA1	40	A	TAA	SAA1	55	A	TAA	SAA1
11	D	TAB	SAB2	26	A	TAA	SAA2	41	B	TAB	SAB1	56	B	TAB	SAB1
12	B	TFA	SFA2	27	B	TFA	SFA2	42	D	TAB	SAB2	57	C	TAA	SAA1
13	B	TFA	SFA2	28	A	TAA	SAA2	43	D	TAB	SAB1	58	B	TAB	SAB2
14	B	TAB	SAB1	29	B	TAA	SAA1	44	C	TAA	SAA1	59	D	TAB	SAB1
15	D	TAA	SAA1	30	C	TAA	SAA1	45	D	TAB	SAB1	60	B	TAB	SAB2

Topics & Subtopics

Code	Description	Code	Description
SAA	General Knowledge	SAB2	Duties
SAA1	Basic Concepts	SCB	Legal
SAA2	Local Issues	SCB2	Rules
SAB	Legal	SFA	Legal
SAB1	Rules	SFA2	Rules

CONTINUE ▶

TEST DIRECTION

DIRECTIONS

Read the questions carefully and then choose the ONE best answer to each question.

Be sure to allocate your time carefully so you are able to complete the entire test within the testing session. You may go back and review your answers at any time.

You may use any available space in your test booklet for scratch work.

Questions in this booklet are not actual test questions but they are the samples for commonly asked questions.

This test aims to cover all topics which may appear on the actual test. However some topics may not be covered.

Studying this booklet will be preparing you for the actual test. It will not guarantee improving your test score but it will help you pass your exam on the first attempt.

Some useful tips for answering multiple choice questions;

- Start with the questions that you can easily answer.

- Underline the keywords in the question.

- Be sure to read all the choices given.

- Watch for keywords such as NOT, always, only, all, never, completely.

- Do not forget to answer every question.

1

Which of the following is the county named in the Venue?

A) The place where the signer personally appeared.
B) The place where the notary's business is located.
C) The place where the signer lives.
D) None of the above

2

If a notary willfully fails to notify the California Secretary of State of a change of address, he or she will be punishable as an infraction by a fine of which of the following?

A) No more than $100
B) No more than $200
C) No more than $500
D) No more than $1,000

3

If you are a new applicant and took an approved six-hour Califorwa notary public education course, which of the following should be included in your application?

A) A check for twenty dollars
B) A 2" x 2" color passport photo
C) A current proof of completion certificate to a new application
D) All of the above

4

It is a fee charged in accordance with any Law. In most cases, this is a fee that is set and approved by a court or a statue.

Which of the following is defined above?

A) Legal fee
B) Statutory Fees
C) Contingency fee
D) Institutional fee

5

When is it not illegal to take an acknowledgment over the telephone?

A) It is always illegal.
B) When the notary has satisfactory evidence that the person making it is the person described
C) When jurat is not required
D) When the venue is not an issue

6

Which of the following refers to the process of proving the genuineness of the signature and seal of a Notary?

A) Apostille
B) Awareness
C) Authentication
D) Attorney in Fact

7

When a signer is physically unable to write his or her signature and can only make an X, the X is called the signer's "mark" and the procedure is called "**signature by mark.**"

For you to notarize such a mark, how many people must watch, or witness, the signer makes his or her mark on the document during the signature by mark process?

A) One

B) Two

C) At least two

D) None of the above

8

Electronic Notarisation (eNotary) can provide a benefit to many industries because of the ability to transfer electronic records quickly.

The rules, requirements and elements of paper-based notarizations apply to eNotary.

Which of the following is/are the elements of eNotary?

A) Electronic Certificate

B) Electronic Document

C) Electronic Signature and Electronic Notary Seal

D) All of the above

9

Notario Público

The problem arises when individuals obtain a notary public license in the United States and use that license to substantiate representations that they are a "**notario publico**" to immigrant populations that ascribe a vastly different meaning to the term.

Which of the following about using the words "notario publico" is correct?

A) It is encouraged

B) It is legal in some states

C) It is prohibited

D) It indicates a lingual ability

10

A **robo-signer** refers to an employee of a mortgage servicing company that signs paperwork such as foreclosure documents robotically without reviewing them. Robo-signers assume the paperwork to be correct and sign it automatically–like robots.

Which of the following about robo-signing to notarize a document is not correct?

A) Robo-signing is an illegal practice in Mortgage Industry.

B) Robo-signing is a failure to require satisfactory evidence of identity with the intend to commit fraud.

C) Robo-signing is a failure to require personal appearance with the intend to commit fraud.

D) All of the above

11

Familiarity with an individual resulting from interactions with that individual over a period of time sufficient to eliminate every reasonable doubt that the individual has the identity claimed.

Which of the following is explained above?

A) Principal

B) Personal know

C) Personal appearance

D) Satisfactory evidence

12

Which of the following refers to the notary wording that contains incorrect information?

A) Protest

B) Deposition

C) False Certificate

D) Notary Misconduct

13

The evidence of a personal debt secured by real property is usually in the form of which of the following?

A) Mortgage

B) Lien

C) Lease

D) Bond

14

The first recognized notary was Tito during the ancient Roman Empire. In ancient Egypt they were known as scribes.

Which of the following about the notaries is a correct statement?

A) Notaries cannot refuse to witness a document based on race, nationality, religion or sex.

B) When performing official notarial acts, Notaries are serving the public service on behalf of their state.

C) A notary is a person authorised to perform acts in legal affairs, in particular witnessing signatures on documents.

D) All of the above

15

In California, which of the following is the fee for administering an oath or affrmation to one person and executing the jurat, including the seal?

A) $2

B) $7

C) $10

D) $15

16

A subscribing witness could also be used in a "Proof of Execution" to swear that "they witnessed another particular person signed a document."

Which of the following can a subscribing witness bring you?

A) Quit Claim Deed

B) Grant Deed

C) Mortgage

D) Homestead Declaration

17

Which of the following is a requirement for becoming a State Notary Public?

A) Being a U.S. citizen or legal permanent resident.

B) Having the equivalent of a "common school education."

C) Being a legal resident of the state or maintaining a business in the state.

D) All of the above

18

Where can a notary get a certificate of authorization from?

A) The governor's office
B) The Department of Real Estate
C) The Secretary of State
D) None of the above

19

If a notary public resigns a position with the employer what must he do?

A) Retake the exam
B) He must resign his commission
C) Notify the Secretary of State of any business address change
D) Leave all journals with the employer for the new notary

20

Notary Public seal must not be surrendered to an employer upon termination of employment, whether or not the employer paid for the seal, or to any other person.

Which of the following is/are correct about notary seal requirements in California?

A) It should be photographically reproducible when affixed to a document.
B) Notaries public may use an embosser seal in addition to the rubber stamp.
C) It should contain the sequential identification number (commission number) assigned to the notary public.
D) All of the above.

21

Within how many days of the filing, a California notary must obtain a new seal that reflects the new name?

A) 5
B) 7
C) 15
D) 30

22

Iis is the individual who has been appointed or reappointed to the office of notary public but has not yet taken the oath of office to be commissioned.

Which of the following is explained above?

A) Appointee
B) Applicant
C) Appoint
D) None of the above

23

It is the portion of a notarized record that is completed by the notary. It bears the notary's signature and seal, and states the facts attested by the notary in a particular notarization.

Which of the following is explained above?

A) Notarial certificate
B) Notarial act
C) Affirmation
D) Acknowledgment

24

Satisfactory evidence would include credible witnesses. A **credible witness** is a person who knows the signer who is willing to swear under oath as to the identity of the signer.

Satisfactory evidence of identity means relying on either which of the following?

A) ID cards
B) Credible identifying witnesses
C) Business card photos
D) Both ID cards and Credible identifying witnesses

25

Which of the following agency of the State gives the new certificate of Notary Public?

A) Corporation Commissioner
B) Bureau of Notary Publics
C) Secretary of State
D) Department of Real Estate

26

A **surety bond** is as a three-party agreement which legally binds together a principal who needs the bond, an obligee who requires the bond and a surety company which sells the bond.

Which of the following about surety bond is correct?

A) It guarantees the principal will act in accordance with certain laws.

B) It protects consumers and government entities from fraud and malpractice.

C) It will cover resulting damages or losses if the principal fails to perform in this manner.

D) All of the above

27

When a notary can not notarize a document?

A) If he is an agent for the document
B) If he is an employer
C) If he is the lawyer for the document
D) If he is trustor or trustee of the document

28

Jurisdiction is the official power to make legal decisions and judgments. After you become a Notary Public, which of the following will be your jurisdiction?

A) The entire State
B) The city in which you work
C) The county in which you live
D) The entire United States

29

Which of the following is signed in the presence of the notary?

A) Certificate
B) Jurat
C) Acknowledgment
D) All of the above

30

Which of the following is a possible size of the stamp?

A) A 6-inches diameter

B) 1 inch in width by 2 ½ inches in length

C) 2 ½ inches by 6 inches

D) One inch square

31

Incumbent means "necessary for someone as a duty or responsibility"

Incumbent comes from the Latin word incumbens, which means lying in or leaning on, but came to mean holding a position. It was first used in English for someone holding a church office, and then someone holding any office.

For which of the following it is incumbent on the notary to scrutinize each document presented?

A) To determine if an oath is required

B) To ensure it is in the form prescribed by law

C) To determine the exact nature of his duty concerning the document

D) To see that the person who executed the instrument has not signed his name without the presence of the notary

32

"**Falsifying documents**" is a type of white-collar crime. It involves altering, changing, or modifying a document to deceive another person. It can also involve the passing along of copies of documents that are known to be false. In many states, falsifying a document is a crime punishable as a felony.

If a notary willingly and knowingly notarizes a real estate document that he knows to be fraudulent, he will be guilty of which of the following?

A) Misdemeanor

B) Lis pendens

C) Statutory crime

D) Felony

33

Notarial act means an action performed by a notary public in his or her official capacity, such as in authenticating a document by witnessing it and placing the notarial seal on it.

Which of the following acts are all Notary Actions?

A) Copy Certification, Acknowledgment, Oath, Deposition

B) Loan Document Signing, Jurat, Affirmation, Protest, Power of Attorney

C) Affidavit, Proof of Execution, Protest, Jurat

D) Acknowledgment, Proof of Execution, Jurat, Oath of Office

34

If a California Notary Public willfully fails to keep his or her notary public seal under the notary public's direct and exclusive control, he or she will be guilty of which of the following?

A) Felony

B) Misdemeanor

C) Official misconduct

D) None of the above

35

When a notary is employed by a city, county or state agency, what happens to the fees collected for non-agency related notarization?

A) It will be kept by the Notary

B) It will be turned over to a supervisor

C) It will be remitted by the Notary Public to the employing agency

D) It will always be free

If a signer of an instrument cannot write (sign) his or her name, that person may sign the document by mark.

Signature by Mark refers to making a mark rather than signing his or her name. To be regarded as a signature, the mark should be witnessed by two persons other than the Notary.

Which of the following is true about the requirements for notarizing a signature by mark in California?

A) According to the Civil Code section 1185, the person signing the document by mark must be identifed by the notary public by satisfactory evidence.

B) The signer's mark must be witnessed by two persons who must subscribe their own names as witnesses on the document.

C) One witness should write the person's name next to the person's mark and then the witness should sign his or her name as a witness.

D) All of the above

It is the completion of a certificate by a notary who has performed a notarial act.

Which of the following is defined above?

A) Attestation

B) Affirmation

C) Commission

D) Acknowledgment

CONTINUE ▶

38

Having a document notarized is the same as swearing under oath in a court of law.

A notary may do which of the following?

A) Notarize friend's documents
B) Notarize a document in a foreign language
C) Refuse to notarize documents that he or she will sign as corporate officers
D) All of the above

39

The **Notary seal** is the impression of the Notary Public inked stamp or crimping embossed and is used to authenticate the Notary's signature and make the notarial act official. The term Notary seal can also refer to your stamp or embosser.

Where do the notaries obtain their seals from?

A) Secretary of State
B) County Clerk
C) Approved vendors or manufacturers
D) Their employer

40

Some states require notaries to keep a notary record book and some states do not; however, all notaries are encouraged to keep a journal of every notarial act.

Which of the following may not be recorded by the notaries in their journals?

A) The date and time of notarization
B) The fees charged for a notarial services
C) Type of the document notarized
D) The signer's address

41

Which of the following may a notary do?

A) Advertise that he is an immigration consultant
B) Take depositions and affidavits
C) Normally notarize a will
D) Certify a copy of a foreign birth certificate

42

It is the security instrument in a loan. It gives the lender a claim against the borrower'(s) home if they default on payment.

Which of the following is explained above?

A) Asset

B) Bond

C) Deed of Trust

D) Power of Attorney

43

Journal of notarial acts refers to the notary public's sequential record of notarial transactions. It is a bound book listing the date, time, and type of each official act. It records the signature of each person whose signature is notarized.

Journal of notarial acts also records the type of information used to verify the identity of parties whose signatures are notarized, and the fee charged. It is also used as evidence in court. Journal of notarial acts is also known as a notarial record, notarial register, or notary record book.

Which of the following is not true about the journal of the notarial act?

A) Some states require a journal's format to include certain features.

B) It contains details of the transaction in the event a notarized document is lost, altered, or if facts concerning the notarization are challenged in court.

C) Most states do not require that Notaries own and maintain a journal or record book of the acts they perform.

D) It is an important tool that provides a written record of the Notary's official acts.

44

A certificate must be included with each notarial act. Which of the following about the certificate is correct?

A) It must be executed at the same time as the performance of the notarial act.

B) It must identify the jurisdiction (state and county) in which the notarial act was performed.

C) It must contain a clear impression of the notary's official stamping device, which includes the commission expiration date.

D) All of the above

45

A notary who is a member of the state bar may take the affidavit of his client concerning any matters when it is taken

A) before a pending cause

B) with the permission of the court of record

C) before the suit commences

D) in his discretion

46

Which of the following is the fee to take an acknowledgment or proof of a deed in California?

A) $7

B) $10

C) $15

D) $25

47

In the law of evidence, a **Credible Witness** is a person making testimony in a court or other tribunal or acting otherwise as a witness, whose credibility is unimpeachable. Several factors affect witnesses' credibility. A credible witness is "**competent to give evidence, and is worthy of belief.**"

Which of the following is correct about Credible Witnesses?

A) They are never placed under oath.

B) They must not have a financial interest in the document.

C) They must always know the notary.

D) All of the above

CONTINUE ▶

Escrow is a legal concept in which a third party holds a financial instrument or an asset on behalf of two other parties that are in the process of completing a transaction.

Escrows should be revocable by which of the following?

A) Either party

B) The escrowee

C) The first party

D) No one needs to know

How many years old must a notary public be at the time of application for appointment?

A) 18

B) 21

C) 23

D) 28

It is the act of taking an acknowledgment, taking a verification or proof or administering an oath or affirmation that a notary is empowered to perform.

Which of the following term defines the process given above?

A) Notary Act

B) Notarial Act

C) Notarization

D) All of the above

1-3/4" Diameter

Notary seal is the impression of the Notary Public inked stamp or crimping embossed and is used to authenticate the Notary's signature and make the notarial act official. The term Notary seal can also refer to your stamp or embosser.

Which of the following about notary seal is correct?

A) It imprints the Notary's name, title (Notary Public) and jurisdiction on a notarized document.

B) It may include such information as the county where the commission and bond are on file.

C) It may include commission number and date of commission expiration.

D) All of the above

CONTINUE ▶

52

The Official Notary seal stamp or seal embosser is the most-used tool of a Notary. The Notary seal is the impression of the Notary Public inked stamp or crimping embossed. It is used to authenticate the Notary's signature and make the notarial act official.

Which of the following is true about an embossed seal impression?

A) It is always required by Notary Law.
B) It can never be used.
C) It is acceptable but not required.
D) It is only for senior notaries.

53

Journal of notarial acts refers to notary public's sequential record of notarial transactions.

Which of the following about the journal is correct?

A) Generally, it is a bound book listing the date, time, and type of each official act.
B) It records the signature of each person whose signature is notarized.
C) It is a detailed, chronological record of the Notary Public's official acts.
D) All of the above

54

In the law of evidence, a **credible witness** is a person making testimony in a court or other tribunal or acting otherwise as a witness, whose credibility is unimpeachable.

Which of the following is true about two credible witnesses?

A) Two credible witnesses are not allowed
B) They must be over 21
C) They must be fingerprinted
D) None of the above

55

It is the empowerment to perform notarial acts and the written evidence of authority to perform those acts.

Which of the following is explained above?

A) Affirmation
B) Attestation
C) Commission
D) Verification

56

A **death certificate** is an official statement, signed by a physician, of the cause, date, and place of a person's death.

Which of the following about death certificate is correct?

A) It must be notarized.

B) It is not notarized.

C) The IRS files it.

D) All of the above

57

Electonic Notary Seal is the private property of the Electronic notary.

The signature and seal of an electronic notary must be secured by which of the following?

A) Token

B) Biometric

C) Password

D) All of the above

58

A **certified copy** is a copy (often a photocopy) of a primary document, that has on it an endorsement or certificate that it is an exact copy of the primary document. It does not certify that the primary document is genuine, only that it is a real copy of the primary document.

Which of the following does a certified copy certify for the reproduction?

A) It states that the reproduction is a real copy of the primary document.

B) It states that the primary document is genuine.

C) It is the same as the original document.

D) None of the above

59

The **unauthorized practice of law** refers to engaging in the practice of law by persons or entities not authorized to practice law according to state law.

Using the designations "lawyer", "attorney at law", "counselor at law," "law", "law office", "J.D." ,"Esq." or other equivalent words by any person or entity who is not authorized is also an unauthorized practice of law.

A Notary who engages in the unauthorized practice of law may face which of the following?

A) Commission denial

B) Commission revocation

C) Commission suspension

D) All of the above

Most U.S. states and jurisdictions only authorize commissioned Notaries Public or other notarial officers recognized under state law to perform notarial acts within the borders of the commissioning state or jurisdiction.

A notary commissioned by the state may perform notarizations anywhere within the state's borders, but may not perform a notarization in another state.

If a notary public moves to another state, where must he apply to be authorized?

A) Secretary of State
B) Notary commission
C) County Clerk
D) Department of Notary Public

Section 3

#	Answer	Topic	Subtopic	#	Answer	Topic	Subtopic	#	Answer	Topic	Subtopic	#	Answer	Topic	Subtopic
1	A	TAA	SAA2	16	D	TAA	SAA1	31	C	TAB	SAB1	46	C	TFA	SFA2
2	C	TFA	SFA2	17	D	TAB	SAB1	32	D	TAB	SAB1	47	B	TAA	SAA2
3	D	TFA	SFA2	18	C	TAB	SAB2	33	D	TAA	SAA2	48	D	TAB	SAB1
4	B	TAA	SAA1	19	C	TAB	SAB2	34	B	TFA	SFA2	49	A	TAB	SAB1
5	A	TAB	SAB2	20	D	TFA	SFA2	35	C	TAB	SAB2	50	D	TAA	SAA2
6	C	TAB	SAB2	21	D	TFA	SFA2	36	D	TFA	SFA2	51	D	TAA	SAA1
7	C	TAB	SAB1	22	A	TAB	SAB1	37	A	TAB	SAB2	52	C	TAA	SAA2
8	D	TAB	SAB3	23	A	TAB	SAB1	38	D	TAB	SAB2	53	D	TAA	SAA1
9	C	TAA	SAA2	24	D	TAB	SAB2	39	C	TAA	SAA2	54	D	TAA	SAA1
10	D	TAB	SAB2	25	C	TAA	SAA2	40	D	TAB	SAB1	55	C	TAB	SAB1
11	B	TAA	SAA1	26	A	TAB	SAB1	41	B	TAA	SAA2	56	B	TAA	SAA1
12	C	TAB	SAB1	27	D	TAB	SAB1	42	C	TAB	SAB2	57	D	TAB	SAB1
13	D	TAA	SAA1	28	A	TAA	SAA2	43	C	TAB	SAB2	58	A	TAA	SAA1
14	D	TAB	SAB2	29	B	TAA	SAA1	44	D	TAA	SAA2	59	D	TAB	SAB2
15	D	TFA	SFA2	30	B	TAA	SAA1	45	D	TAA	SAA1	60	A	TAA	SAA2

Topics & Subtopics

Code	Description	Code	Description
SAA	General Knowledge	SAB2	Duties
SAA1	Basic Concepts	SAB3	eNotary
SAA2	Local Issues	SFA	Legal
SAB	Legal	SFA2	Rules
SAB1	Rules		

CONTINUE ▶

Made in the USA
Las Vegas, NV
03 October 2021